World Ci

SYDNEY

Christine Hatt

Belitha Press

First published in the UK in 1999 by
Belitha Press Limited
London House, Great Eastern Wharf,
Parkgate Road, London SW11 4NQ

ISBN 1 84138 017 2

British Library Cataloguing in Publication Data
for this book is available from the British Library.

Printed in Singapore

Editor Stephanie Bellwood
Designer Hayley Cove
Map illustrator Lorraine Harrison
Picture researcher Kathy Lockley
Consultant Professor Carl Bridge,
Robert Menzies Centre for Australian Studies
Educational consultant Elizabeth Lewis

Picture acknowledgements
Associated Press Picture Library : 41tl. Australian Picture Library : Cover tr, 30, /Barbara Zussine 13, /Charbaux 27, /Craig Lamotte 12b, 42, /D & J Heaton 15tr, /Dave Morgan 28tl, /David Ball 34tr, /Eric Sierins 31tr, /Esther Beaton 35tl, /Flying Photos 37tr, /J. Carnemolla 4, 5b, 12t, 22tl, 23t, 24-5b, 26b, 29tl, 38b, 38t, 39t, 39b, /Jonathan Marks 16t, 18, 21cr, /JP & ES Baker 17bl, /Nick Rains 15bl, 43br, /Oliver Strewe 15tl, 36tr, /Peter Brennan 5t, / R. Garvey 11b, /Steve Vidler 19bl, /Strawberry Col. 23b. Coo-ee Historical Picture Library : 8, 9b, 9t, 10b, 10t, 11t, 26t, 40tr. Robert Harding Picture Library : Cover b, 1, 14, 19tr, 20t, 24, 28br, 33bl, 34bl, 36bl. Hogarth Galleries Pty. Ltd., Aboriginal Art Centres: Cover: tl, 35br. Art Gallery of New South Wales, Mollie Gowing Acquisition Fund for Contemporary Aboriginal Art 1996 /© courtesy Anthony Wallis, Aboriginal Artists Agency Ltd., Sydney: CLIFFORD POSSUM TJAPALTJARRI, *Lungkata's two sons at Warlugulong*, 1976, synthetic polymer paint on canvas board, 70.5 x 55.0 cm: 33tr. N.H.P.A. /A.N.T: 16b, 17tr. Rex Features: 21tl, 29cr, 37bl, 40bl, 41br, 43tl. Wildlight Photo Agency: /Andrew Rankin 22cr, /Philip Quirk 20bl, 31bl, 32.

Words in **bold** are explained in the glossary on pages 46 and 47.

CONTENTS

INTRODUCTION

The city of Sydney lies on the south-eastern coast of Australia, on either side of a spectacular harbour that leads into the brilliant blue waters of the Pacific Ocean. Sydney is Australia's largest and oldest city, founded in 1788. Its central area covers just over six square kilometres. Suburbs sprawl to the north, south and west to give Sydney a total area of about 12,407 square kilometres. About 3.8 million people, known as Sydneysiders, live within its borders.

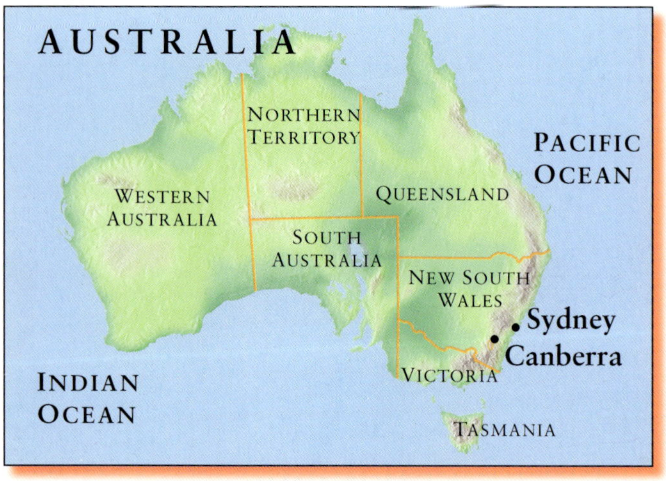

Early settlers were stunned by the beauty of Sydney's harbour. Today, with its many tall buildings and its famous bridge, it is still breathtaking.

Pacific port

Sydney has become a major port for both passenger and cargo ships. Many luxury liners moor at Darling Harbour and Circular Quay, in the main Sydney Harbour area. Most **container ships**, which carry goods to and from places all over the world, dock further south, in Botany Bay. Sydney is also the most important base of the Royal Australian Navy. Its ships cluster around the navy headquarters on Garden Island.

FAST FACTS

SYDNEY

STATUS

Capital of **state** of New South Wales (NSW)

AREA

12,407 square kilometres

POPULATION

3,880,000 (1997)

GOVERNING BODY

State government and local councils, including the City Council of Sydney

CLIMATE

Temperatures average 26°C in February and 16°C in July

TIME ZONE

Greenwich Mean Time plus 10 hours

CURRENCY

1 Australian dollar (A$) = 100 cents

OFFICIAL LANGUAGE

English

Leisurely lifestyle

Sydney's location has helped to create the city's special way of life. Many Sydneysiders regularly visit the harbour beaches, as well as the 60 km of Pacific coastline. Swimming, surfing, sailing and other water sports are all popular and people spend many hours outside. Sydney's climate makes this outdoor lifestyle possible. Summers (December to February) are warm and sunny, while winters (June to August) are usually mild. But there are occasional downpours, and sometimes a strong summer wind, the Southerly Buster, blows through the city.

A container ship waits in the terminal at Botany Bay. Cargo is packed into straight-sided containers like those on the deck.

The City Council of Sydney meets in Sydney Town Hall. It is one of many local councils in the city and controls only about six square kilometres of land.

State capital

Sydney is the capital of New South Wales, one of Australia's six states. The state parliament meets in the city. It controls some aspects of Sydney life, such as schools and railways. Local councils and other special organizations look after matters such as parks, roads and libraries.

MAPS OF THE CITY

These maps show you Sydney as it is today. The area map shows Sydney's vast suburbs and Pacific beaches, and the street map gives a closer view of the city centre. Many of the places mentioned in the book are marked.

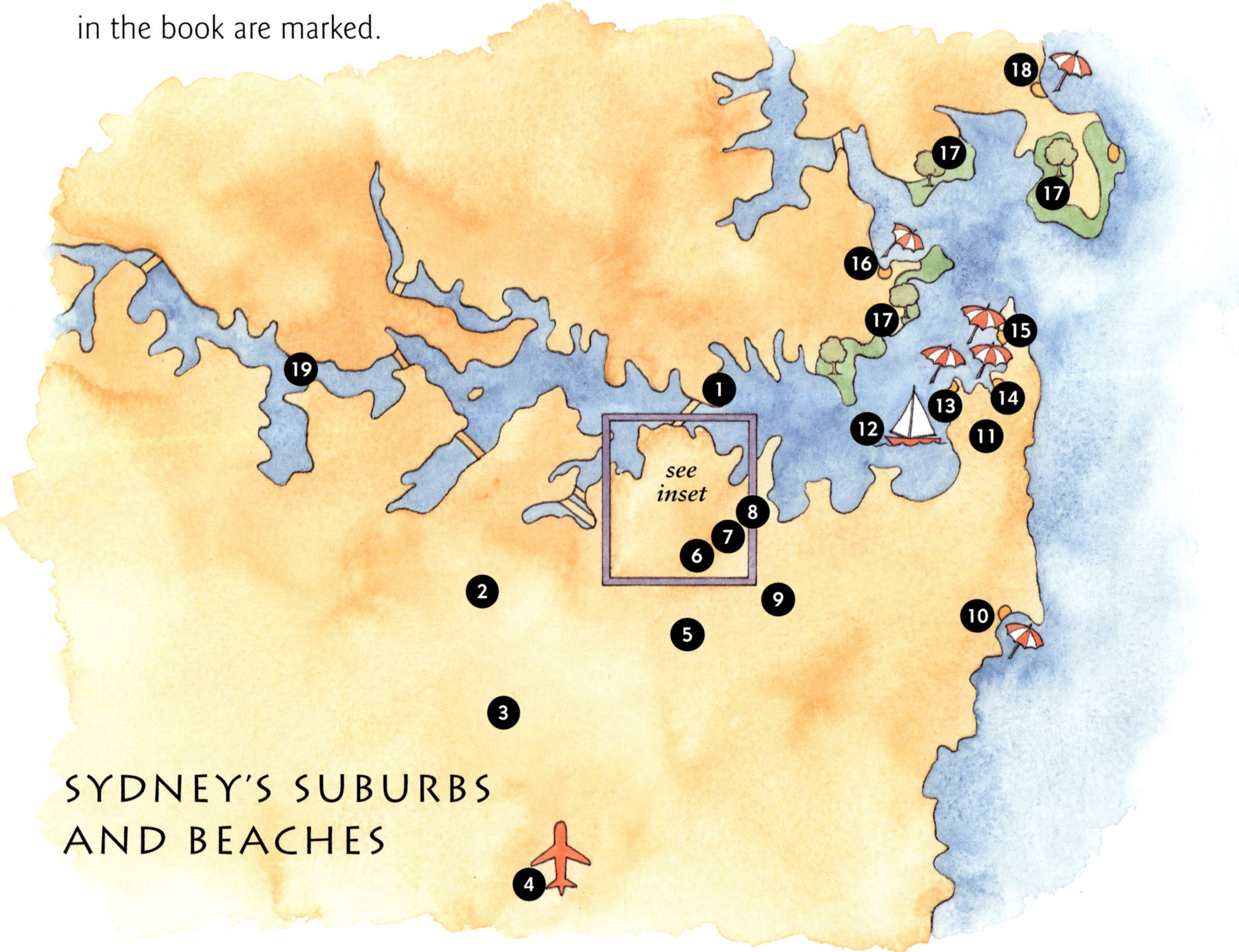

1 Kirribilli
2 Leichhardt
3 Marrickville
4 Kingsford Smith Airport
5 Redfern
6 Surry Hills
7 Darlinghurst
8 Kings Cross
9 Paddington
10 Bondi Beach
11 Vaucluse
12 Sydney Harbour (Port Jackson)
13 Shark Bay
14 Parsley Bay
15 Watsons Bay
16 Balmoral
17 Sydney Harbour National Park
18 Manly
19 Parramatta River

1. Powerhouse Museum
2. Chinatown
3. Chinese Garden
4. Darling Harbour
5. Sydney Town Hall
6. Queen Victoria Building
7. State Theatre
8. Great Synagogue
9. Anzac Memorial
10. Australian Museum
11. St Mary's Cathedral
12. Hyde Park
13. Sydney Tower
14. St James' Church
15. Hyde Park Barracks
16. Art Gallery of NSW
17. The Domain
18. State Parliament House
19. Museum of Sydney
20. Royal Botanic Gardens
21. Justice and Police Museum
22. Circular Quay
23. Museum of Contemporary Art
24. Sydney Observatory
25. Cadman's Cottage
26. Central Business District
27. Sydney Opera House
28. Sydney Harbour Tunnel
29. Sydney Harbour Bridge

CENTRAL SYDNEY

SYDNEY'S EARLY HISTORY

Australia's first inhabitants were the Aborigines, who arrived from South-East Asia at least 40,000 years ago. Aboriginal tribes gradually spread south and about 20,000 years later had reached the area that is now Sydney Harbour. The main Aboriginal tribe there was the Iora. Its members lived in caves or bark huts. They ate mostly fish and shellfish, but also hunted animals and gathered plants, birds' eggs and honey.

Captain Phillip raised the Union Jack ➤ at Sydney Cove on 26 January 1788. This is an early 20th-century painting of the flag-raising scene.

Captain Cook

The Aborigines probably met no one from outside Australia for thousands of years. Then, on 29 April 1770, English explorer Captain James Cook and his crew landed in Botany Bay, 16 km south of Sydney Harbour. The Aborigines threw spears at the strangers, then ran off into the bush. The Europeans studied the bay before making their way up Australia's east coast, which they claimed for Britain and named New South Wales.

Penal colony

In 1786 the British government decided to set up a **penal colony** in Botany Bay. On 13 May 1787 the First Fleet of 11 ships set sail for Australia. On board were its leader, Captain Arthur Phillip, more than 700 soldiers and sailors with their families, and 736 convicts. The fleet arrived in January 1788, but the bay's poor soil and lack of fresh water made it unsuitable for settlement. So Captain Phillip sailed north and found a better harbour – Sydney Cove.

A hard life

Conditions in the penal colony were harsh. Convicts toiled under the hot sun to build huts, first from wood and mud, then from brick. They also planted crops, but these did not grow well. The newcomers almost starved before the Second Fleet arrived with food in 1790. Meanwhile, relations between Europeans and Aborigines grew more hostile.

▼ A small group of Aborigines (bottom left) looks on as the Sydney settlement grows. This picture dates from 1802.

The making of a city

The settlement slowly grew. It soon contained not only convicts but also free settlers, who began to arrive in 1793. Then, in 1810, a dynamic Scot called Lachlan Macquarie became Governor of New South Wales. He worked with the convict architect Francis Greenway (see page 40) to construct roads and public buildings. By the end of his 11-year rule, Sydney was a true city. In 1813 explorers crossed the Blue Mountains west of Sydney and discovered vast grasslands. Soon thousands more free settlers arrived to set up sheep farms there, and wool became a major export.

Governor Lachlan Macquarie was an ▲ army officer who had worked in both India and the Middle East before setting out for Sydney with his wife.

A new era

By 1840 about 83,000 convicts had been shipped to Sydney. About 70,000 free settlers had also made their way to the city. In that year the British stopped sending criminals to New South Wales, and a new era in the city's life began.

SYDNEY FROM THE 1840S

Sydney was officially declared a city in 1842 when it had a population of about 60,000. Then, in 1851, gold was discovered west of the Blue Mountains. **Prospectors** rushed to the region, and by 1890 about 400,000 people lived in the city.

◄ Men pan for gold in the Ophir Goldfields west of Sydney. Many thousands went to the site in the 1850s, but few made their fortunes.

Trading wealth

Population growth and trade in wool and wheat turned Sydney into a wealthy community. Men paved the city's dusty streets with wood and constructed solid buildings that showed its new status. Among them were the Customs House (1887) and the Town Hall (1889).

Poverty and crime

There was poverty too. Many people lived in slums, especially in the Rocks district near the harbour, where gangs of thieves roamed. In 1900 rats spread plague through the city, and 112 people died. The rats were killed and the slums cleared to prevent further outbreaks.

Political change

In 1855 Sydney politicians set up a parliament, and in 1856 the city became capital of the New South Wales colony. In 1901, New South Wales joined five other colonies to form Australia and became a **state** of this new nation. Sydney became the state capital.

The First World War

Many Sydney citizens fought in the **First World War** (1914-18), most famously at Gallipoli in Turkey. The Anzac Memorial in Sydney's Hyde Park commemorates them. After the war, in the early 1930s, economic **depression** struck Sydney. Unemployment soared, but the wool trade recovered and new industries grew.

Australian soldiers in the trenches at Gallipoli, where they fought from 1915-16. The ill-planned attack cost 36,000 lives. ▼

The Second World War

Sydneysiders also fought in the **Second World War** (1939-45), both overseas and at home. On 31 May 1942 three Japanese submarines sailed into Sydney Harbour to attack an American ship. They did not reach their target and were sunk.

Immigration and expansion

After the war, in 1947, the Australian government encouraged immigration to provide skilled workers for industry. Thousands of people from many countries poured into Sydney. The city has continued to grow ever since. In 1988 Sydney celebrated its 200th anniversary and in 2000 the city will host the Olympic Games.

◄ The Sydney of 1802 (see page 9) is no longer recognizable in this 1905 photo. In 100 years the settlement had become an impressive city.

CENTENARY CELEBRATIONS

When Sydney celebrated its first centenary (100th birthday) in 1888, there were joyful street parades and a **regatta** in the harbour. A new park, Centennial Park, was opened. Thirteen years later, the ceremony to mark the birth of Australia was held there. When Sydney reached 200, the festivities were even more magnificent. On 26 January 1988, ships re-enacted the arrival of the First Fleet, while Sydneysiders enjoyed all sorts of entertainments, from street parades to orchestral concerts. In the evening a stunning firework display (above) filled the sky.

THE PEOPLE OF SYDNEY

Most of the early settlers in Sydney were British or Irish. By the end of the **Second World War**, these two groups still formed about 95 per cent of the population. But the immigration policy introduced by the government after the war (see page 11) has transformed Sydney into a truly multicultural city.

Football fans in the suburb of Leichhardt show their support for the Italian team in the 1998 World Cup.

New arrivals

The first post-war immigrants to arrive were from Europe, especially Greece, Italy, Turkey and Yugoslavia. Members of each nationality stayed together and set up communities. Many Greeks, for example, settled in the suburb of Marrickville.

Different peoples

At first, the national government encouraged only white Europeans to come to Australia, but in the 1960s Asian people began to arrive. In 1976 many Lebanese people came to Sydney, escaping from civil war at home. Refugees from war in Vietnam and Cambodia soon followed. In the 1990s, large numbers of Hong Kong Chinese also arrived. They joined Chinese communities that had existed since the gold rush, when hundreds of **prospectors** had come to Sydney from China.

This ornate gateway marks the entrance to Dixon Street, an area in the Chinatown district of Sydney.

Religious life

Most early Sydneysiders were Christians: either British Protestants or Irish Roman Catholics. By the late 19th century there were two cathedrals in the city, St Andrew's for **Anglican** worshippers and St Mary's for Catholics. Today the city contains many other Christian groups, too, including a large Greek Orthodox community. About 35,000 Jews live in modern Sydney and many worship in the Great Synagogue. There are thousands of Muslims in the city too, many of whose families came from Turkey and the Lebanon. There are several mosques for worship.

Harmony and racism

The Australian government promotes racial harmony and in 1989 published its *National Agenda for a Multicultural Australia*. But there is still racism in the country. One parliament member in particular, Pauline Hanson of the One Nation Party, stirred up feeling against Asians and Aborigines. She lost her seat in the 1998 elections. Targets of racist abuse in Sydney include Lebanese, Chinese and Aboriginal people.

THE ABORIGINES

Fifty years after the first convicts arrived in Sydney, almost all the Iora Aborigines (see pages 8-9) had died. Many were killed by European diseases such as cholera, to which they had no immunity. Other Aborigines moved into the city, but the settlers destroyed their way of life, took their land and forced them to live on **reserves**. Today Aborigines make up only 0.6 per cent of Sydney's population. Most of them live in the suburbs of Redfern (see page 21) and La Perouse. Many have poor housing and little money. But a strong Aboriginal rights movement has emerged. This amazing *Sea of Hands* display (left) was put up on Bondi Beach in 1998 to draw attention to Aborigines' claims for justice.

BUILDINGS AND BRIDGES

Sydney's two world-famous landmarks – Sydney Harbour Bridge and Sydney Opera House – make the city instantly recognizable. But a trip through the streets reveals many other impressive buildings.

Spotlights pick out Sydney Opera House and Sydney Harbour Bridge at night, creating a spectacular scene. ▼

Sydney Harbour Bridge

In Sydney's early years, the only way to cross from the north to the south shore of the city was to take a ferry across the water. Then, in 1932, Sydney Harbour Bridge opened. Its magnificent arch is 503m long and contains more than 50,000 tonnes of steel. Sydneysiders call it the Coat Hanger because of its shape. The bridge carries six lanes of traffic, two railway lines, a cycle track and a footpath. About 150,000 vehicles use the bridge every day, and must pay a toll (fee).

The Opera House

In 1955 the Sydney authorities decided to build a new concert hall. They organized an international competition for architects. The winning plan was the spectacular shell design of Danish architect Jørn Utzon. There were many difficulties during construction, but Sydney Opera House was eventually opened by Queen Elizabeth II in 1973. The magnificent structure, which stands on Bennelong Point at the very edge of the harbour, contains not only an opera theatre, but also three other concert halls, restaurants and bars.

◄ Visitors to the Hyde Park Barracks museum can sleep in hammocks there overnight, just as convicts once did.

The thin column of Sydney Tower is held firmly in place by 56 massive steel cables. ►

Macquarie Street

Macquarie Street was a dirt track until Lachlan Macquarie (see pages 8-9) turned it into an elegant road. Its fine buildings include the Hyde Park Barracks (1819). This once housed 600 convicts but now contains a museum of convict life. The city's oldest church, St James' Church (1820), is also on the street. The copper on its roof was marked with arrows so that if convicts stole it, the metal could be identified and returned. Here, too, are State Parliament House, where people can watch political debates, and the State Library of New South Wales.

THE ROCKS

The harbourside Rocks area, so called because of its rocky shoreline, was where Sydney's first settlers lived. Since the 1970s many of its old buildings have been restored. Now it attracts tourists eager to learn about the city's origins. Among the sights is Cadman's Cottage (below). It was built in 1816 and is the oldest surviving building in central Sydney. Nearby Sydney Observatory (1858) was where astronomers used to study the heavens. Today it is a popular astronomy museum.

Sydney Tower

Sydney Tower was completed in 1981. It is 305m tall, the highest building in the city. The view from the observation platform at the top is truly breathtaking. Visitors can see the harbour area, Botany Bay to the south and sometimes the Blue Mountains, far to the west. In 1998 three giant steel sculptures of athletes were placed on top of the tower. They will be there until the end of the 2000 Olympic Games.

PARKS AND GARDENS

Sydney has many large parks where people can relax and shelter from the heat under shady trees. The city is also surrounded by huge national parks, whose land and wildlife is protected by the **state**.

▲ The Royal Botanic Gardens were founded in 1856, but the Pyramid glasshouse was built during the 1970s.

The Royal Botanic Gardens

The 30-hectare Royal Botanic Gardens overlook Sydney Harbour. This is where convicts grew vegetables on Australia's first farm. Today the gardens contain plants such as fig and eucalyptus trees. Special sites in the park include the Sydney Tropical Centre. Inside its huge glasshouses gardeners have created a mini-rainforest. The National **Herbarium** of New South Wales is also in the Gardens.

NATIONAL PARKS

Sydney has ten national parks. Sydney Harbour National Park is made up of seven separate harbourside locations, as well as Clark, Shark and Rodd Islands. The other parks are far away from the city. The largest is the Royal National Park, to the south. It is mainly heathland, but also contains forests and sandy beaches. Ku-ring-gai Chase National Park, to the north, is the place to see Aboriginal rock art. Walkers have to watch out for poisonous spiders such as the Red Back (right).

Plants from both China and Australia surround the pavilion in Sydney's Chinese Garden. They are intended to be living signs of the two countries' friendship. ➤

The Domain

The Domain is a park next to the Botanic Gardens. Here people can visit the Andrew 'Boy' Charlton swimming pool and the Art Gallery of New South Wales. The Domain hosts open-air classical concerts in January, the middle of Australia's summer. People come to the park on Sundays to express their views. Crowds gather to listen – and to shout back if they disagree. This tradition began in the late 19th century and since then there have been some eccentric speakers, for example a man who dressed as an ancient Roman.

Taronga Zoo runs programmes to breed endangered species such as red pandas (below) and snow leopards.

Taronga Zoo

Taronga Zoo was set up on Sydney's north shore in 1916. Today its 30 hectares house more than 3,500 animals. Many of these, such as koalas and wombats, live only in Australia. Moats rather than cages are used to keep people and dangerous animals apart. There are also opportunities to get close to the zoo's friendlier creatures. In the Australian Walkabout section visitors can wander among wallabies and kangaroos.

The Chinese Garden

Sydney has links with a Chinese city called Guangzhou. Landscape architects from this city designed the Chinese Garden, also known as the Garden of Friendship, in Darling Harbour. The garden contains many Chinese features, including jasmine bushes, weeping willow trees, a **pavilion** and a lake filled with koi carp. Visitors can drink Chinese tea in the garden teahouse.

BAYS AND BEACHES

The uneven coastline of Sydney Harbour has hundreds of beautiful bays with long beaches of yellow and white sand. Sydneysiders head for the beaches at every opportunity – not only at weekends, but also after a long day in the factory or office. They go to swim, sail or simply to enjoy the sunshine and the view.

▲ A few bathers wade into the tranquil water of Watsons Bay, while less energetic people prefer to laze on the golden beach.

Harbour beaches

One of the most famous harbour beaches is Watsons Bay, on the south shore. It was once a small fishing village, but has now become a favourite spot for family picnics and seafood restaurants (see page 37). Some of the most popular beaches are Parsley Bay and Shark Bay, in the wealthy area of Vaucluse. One of the best beaches on the north shore is Balmoral, where the swimming is safe for children, and fish and chip shops line the waterfront. The waves are not large enough for surfing anywhere in the harbour, which is why many Sydneysiders make their way to the Pacific Ocean.

BEACH SAFETY

There are drawbacks to Sydney's seaside lifestyle. The ocean's powerful currents can be deadly, so trained lifesavers patrol many beaches. They use flags to mark areas where it is safe to swim and keep a lookout for anyone in trouble. They also watch out for sharks, which occasionally attack ocean swimmers or make their way into the harbour. For this reason, many harbour bays contain protected swimming areas that are enclosed by shark nets.

The popularity of Bondi Beach ▼ often leads to overcrowding, as well as litter on the sand and in the streets nearby.

Bondi Beach

The Pacific beach closest to central Sydney is the world-famous Bondi Beach, to the south. Its towering breakers and 1km-long expanse of soft sand attract surfers from all over the world, as well as swimmers and sunbathers.

▼ Manly's main pedestrian area, The Corso, contains many shops and restaurants, as well as a street market at weekends.

Surfing paradise

The most famous surfing beach on the Pacific coast north of Sydney was named by Captain Arthur Phillip (see page 8). He called it Manly because he thought the Aborigines who lived there were just that. Today Manly is a very popular resort. As well as two beaches, it has a funfair and a giant aquarium called Oceanworld.

HOMES AND HOUSING

In the early 19th century, the main part of Sydney was around the harbour. But the city quickly spread, especially after the gold rush of the 1850s (see pages 10-11). Most settlers wanted to build a house of their own, so they added suburb after suburb to the city. As a result, Sydney expanded south, north and west, then along the Pacific coast. Now the city has about 600 suburbs.

Paddington houses such as these, with their delicate ironwork balconies, are protected by the Australian National Trust. ▲

Paddington

Paddington, popularly known as Paddo, is one of Sydney's most famous inner suburbs. It is east of the centre and contains rows of 19th-century terraced houses. Many have balconies made of 'Sydney lace' ironwork, featuring designs of Australian plants and animals. Paddington was once a poor area, but is now fashionable.

OUTER SUBURBS

Most Sydneysiders do not live in the terraces and flats of the inner suburbs. Instead, they inhabit sprawling outer suburbs such as Sylvania Waters in the south-west (left). Here the most common homes are cement- or brick-walled bungalows with red-tiled roofs. Many have a garden, a garage and a swimming pool attached. Some people complain that the outer suburbs are all the same and have no character. But they provide decent, affordable housing for many thousands of Sydneysiders.

▲ Aboriginal paintings cover the side of a house in this Redfern street. The poverty of the surroundings is clear to see.

Redfern

The inner suburb of Redfern lies south of the city centre. Many Aborigines who came to Sydney from other parts of Australia settled there and created their own style of housing. They painted the outsides of existing terraced houses in the reds and browns of traditional Aboriginal art. They also knocked down walls inside to make large rooms where **extended families** could live together. Now Redfern is changing as developers renovate houses and sell them at high prices. Soon Aborigines and other poor Redfern residents may be forced out.

Kirribilli

The small suburb of Kirribilli, on Sydney's north shore, is the most densely populated in the city. Like other inner suburbs, it contains many high-rise blocks divided into flats, known as home units. It also has many luxurious harbourside mansions owned by rich business people. Kirribilli House, the Australian Prime Minister's Sydney home, and Admiralty House, where Australia's **Governor-General** lives, are also in Kirribilli.

Sydney Harbour ▲ Bridge can be glimpsed behind the tower blocks of Kirribilli in this waterside scene.

Federation Style

When Australia was founded in 1901 (see page 10), its six **states** joined in a **federation**. Soon afterwards, many Sydney homes were built in the new Federation Style of architecture. Features of the style include tiled roofs, **gables**, verandahs and stained-glass windows. The southern suburb of Haberfield is filled with bungalows of this type, which is why it is known as the Federation Suburb.

EDUCATION

In Australia every **state** provides children with both primary and secondary education. Children in New South Wales must attend school from six to fifteen. Some children start pre-school education at three and many continue their education until they are sixteen or eighteen. Most pupils go to government-funded schools, but in Sydney there are also private schools. Pupils in both types of school usually wear uniform.

▲ A group of Sydney primary school children. Some of the boys are wearing legionnaire's caps to protect their necks from the sun.

Curriculum choices

The Australian curriculum has eight key areas of learning: English, mathematics, technology, science, studies of society and the environment, arts, health and languages other than English.

Pupils in a Sydney classroom ▲ working on computers. Australian schoolchildren learn how to use computers at an early age.

Languages

Language-learning is especially encouraged in Australia, both to help students from non-English backgrounds keep in touch with their own cultures and to teach Australians languages that they may need for business. The most popular non-English language is Italian, but Chinese, Japanese, Korean and Indonesian are also taught. In suburbs such as Redfern, Aboriginal pupils are taught their own languages.

The main campus of the University of Sydney, near the city centre, contains many old stone buildings and grassy **quadrangles**.

Further education

Almost a third of Australians go on to further education, which is funded by the federal (national) government. Sydney has five public universities. The oldest is the University of Sydney, founded in 1850. Specialist colleges of this university are scattered across the city. The **Conservatorium** of Music, for example, is in the Royal Botanic Gardens (see page 16). Other universities include the University of New South Wales, Macquarie University and the University of Western Sydney, which has five separate campuses.

OVERSEAS STUDENTS

Sydney universities educate Australians from a wide variety of **ethnic** backgrounds. Since the 1980s, overseas students have also been actively encouraged to enrol at the city's universities. Many thousands have done so. The vast majority of these students are from **Asia-Pacific countries** such as Indonesia and Malaysia.

INDUSTRY AND FINANCE

Sydney's first major industry was whaling, but the sale and export of wool and wheat soon became much more important (see page 10). In 1890 and again in the 1930s, economic **depression** hit the city. Since those difficult years, Sydney has steadily grown to become a major industrial and business centre with links right across the world.

The skyscrapers of Sydney's **Central Business District** contain thousands of busy people hoping to make successful deals and large amounts of money. ▼

Sydney's industries

About a third of Sydney's workers have jobs in manufacturing industries. The goods they make include office machinery, electrical equipment, clothes and processed food. Most Sydneysiders work in service industries such as entertainment, the retail trade, tourism and finance. Tourism is Sydney's fastest-growing industry. In 1995 more than 1.6 million tourists visited the city and this number is likely to double both during and after the 2000 Olympic Games (see pages 42-43).

THE NEWSPAPER INDUSTRY

Sydney is the headquarters of News Corporation, a worldwide media business run by tycoon Rupert Murdoch. It publishes *The Australian*, *The Daily Telegraph Mirror* and *Sunday Telegraph*. News Corporation's main rival in Sydney is the Fairfax group. It publishes *The Sydney Morning Herald*. Material from these newspapers is also available on-line (right). The biggest magazine publisher in the city is Australian Consolidated Press, owned by super-rich businessman Kerry Packer. Its best-known publications include *Australian Women's Weekly*, and *Bulletin*, a current affairs magazine.

Netscape: The Sydney Morning Herald

Back Forward Reload Home Search Guide Images Print Security Stop

Netsite: http://www.smh.com.au/

BREAKING NEWS

Weekdays from mid-morning

TEXT INDEX

THE TRADING ROOM

1998 SYDNEY MOTOR SHOW

IT JOBS & NEWS

The Sydney Morning Herald

TODAY'S NEWS

Monday, October 26, 1998

Exploited children: the brutal truth

More than 1,600 child workers, some as young as 12, are being seriously injured or maimed each year in Australia. Full story

Showdown with militants looms

The Israeli Prime Minister, Mr Netanyahu, and the Palestinian leader, Mr Arafat, are preparing for a possible showdown with militants in their camps, who threaten to derail the latest land-for-security deal. Full story

Habibie's challenge

In the first article of a five-part series on the state of Indonesia, Asia Editor DAVID JENKINS asks if President B.J. Habibie has what it takes to pull his nation back from the precipice. Full story

PAGE ONE: Special report - Children for hire; The tax-cut path to 5% jobless rate; Mob rule in Indonesia, a nation ripe for revolution.

NATIONAL: Utzon offered final say on interior redesign; Kakadu's heritage listing at risk; Blast for mining finance bosses; Poles salute Tobruk heroes; Revolt over HSC honours list.

WORLD: Another warning for tardy Milosevic; Diana 'the first to have affair'; Police turn up the heat on Anwar rallies; Court orders tally of Murdoch assets.

BUSINESS: Markets on alert for CPI; Brierley the key as Quek's dragon loses its puff; Rivals move on Blom's Cinema Plus shares; Rags-and-riches drama drags on at Country Road; Mixed call on customer support.

SPORT: Six reasons why England can win the Ashes - and six why

DOCK OF THE BAY

Hasselhoff

Full Story

TEST CRICKET

Australia v Pakistan

Live coverage

Sydney 2000

OLYMPIC COUNTDOWN

All the latest news leading up to the Sydney 2000

Twin ports

Two container ports, in Sydney Harbour and Botany Bay, handle most of Australia's imports and exports. In 1997 they processed more than 21 million tonnes of goods. Coal, wool and beef are exported, as well as manufactured goods. Major imports are cars and **crude petroleum**. Japan buys more Australian and New South Wales exports than any other country.

Business and banking

Sydney's Central Business District (CBD) and its smaller equivalent in North Sydney make up the most important financial centre in Australia. Smartly dressed men and women work in its skyscrapers for the country's leading businesses, banks and law firms from early in the morning until late at night. 39 banks, including the mighty Westpac Banking Corporation, have their headquarters in the city, as well as 60 of Australia's top 100 companies. The city is also the main base of the Reserve Bank of Australia, which issues the country's bank notes, and of the Australian Stock Exchange.

◄ The Sydney Convention and Exhibition Centre opened in Darling Harbour in 1988. Companies attend trade fairs in its five halls, which can be linked to form one huge area.

CRIME AND PUNISHMENT

Street and house burglary were common in early Sydney. By the late 19th century, gangs of thugs known as larrikins roamed the city, terrorizing its inhabitants. They committed many serious crimes, including murder. Bushrangers (highwaymen) such as Jack Donahoe and Mad-Dog Morgan lived on the outskirts of Sydney and made a living by stealing from the rich.

◀ Bushrangers lie in wait for a mail coach in the 19th century. Many of the first bushrangers were runaway convicts.

▼ Sydney is quite a safe city, where serious crimes are rare. Police officers like these are available to help anyone who needs them.

Sydney police

There are several separate police forces in Australia. The Australian Federal Police are based in the national capital, Canberra. They deal with major crime that crosses **state** boundaries, such as drug smuggling. New South Wales and every other state operates its own police force to deal with local crimes. In Sydney, both male and female police officers wear a blue uniform with a hat, and are usually armed. They generally make foot patrols around the city in teams of two. To move around more quickly they use either motorbikes or vans equipped with flashing lights.

JUSTICE AND POLICE MUSEUM

Sydney's Justice and Police Museum is near the Rocks area of the city (see page 15), where many larrikins used to lurk. Here you can examine photographs and **plaster casts** of notorious Sydney criminals, as well as some of the terrifying weapons that they used. You can also see a restored **charge room** and magistrates' court, or even step into a gloomy prison cell.

Sydney Aborigines and their supporters march through the city to protest against the large number of Aborigine deaths in police custody.

Common crimes

Today theft is the most common crime in Sydney – pickpockets are active in rough areas such as Kings Cross and in crowded tourist sites. Police advise people to leave their valuables at home or in their hotel. Drug-taking is also quite widespread. Possession of even small amounts of illegal substances can lead to a jail sentence. Murders in Sydney are very rare – there are about two for every 100,000 Sydneysiders.

Organized crime

Organized gangs have operated in Sydney for years. They arrange crimes and run illegal businesses such as drug-dealing and gambling. As new communities arrive, new gangs emerge, including Chinese **Triads**. In the mid-1980s, gang warfare resulted in street shootings. An investigation found police corruption and involvement with criminals. The police are trying to improve their image, but many still do not trust them.

Aboriginal arrests

Aborigines are about 20 times more likely to be arrested and imprisoned than non-Aborigines. Aboriginal deaths in police custody are also high – in the early 1990s there was one every two weeks. Police brutality, fuelled by racism, was suspected in many cases. In 1991 a **Royal Commission** report listed more than 300 ways to improve the situation and police now attend programmes which aim to eliminate racist attitudes.

GETTING AROUND

Sydney's location on two shores of a harbour, plus its huge network of suburbs, mean that a good transport system is vital. Early Sydneysiders travelled by horse-drawn carriage, tram or steam ferry. In the mid-19th century the railway arrived, and in the 20th century people began to use cars. Now there is a great variety of ways to get around.

▲ This is the famous Indian-Pacific train that carries passengers from Sydney to Perth in Western Australia in 65 hours.

Train travel

Rail travel within Sydney is provided mainly by the CityRail system, which runs underground in the city centre. Its double-decker trains speed along six lines that extend far into the suburbs. A new Light Rail line runs from the city to the west, and a second line to link the centre with eastern suburbs is being built. Trains to other parts of Australia leave from the Central Railway Station.

MONORAIL MAGIC

Sydney's **monorail** (below) makes a regular round trip from the city centre to the tourist haven of Darling Harbour. There are just seven stops on its three-and-a-half kilometre raised track, so it is of little use to most Sydneysiders. But it does offer visitors wonderful views of the harbour and attractions such as Sydney Tower.

On the bus

There are three main types of bus in Sydney, all single-deckers. Blue and white buses operate on a wide range of routes in the centre of the city. Red Explorer buses make trips around 22 tourist sites, while blue-striped Bondi and Bay Explorers head for the beaches.

◄ To catch a water taxi, people simply raise an arm as though they are trying to stop a bus.

Ferries and water taxis

Travelling by water makes sense in a harbourside city. Ferries travel from Circular Quay to more than 30 places, including Manly and Taronga Zoo. Passengers can travel on a standard ferry or a much quicker JetCat. People also hail water taxis, which take them wherever they want to go – at a price.

Traffic congestion ► is a very common sight nowadays on Sydney Harbour Bridge, especially in the early evening as people travel home from work.

Air travel

Sydney's airport, north of Botany Bay, is called Kingsford Smith Airport. It is the busiest in Australia for internal and international flights. In 1994 a third runway was opened to cope with all the traffic. The airport is named after Sir Charles Kingsford Smith, a famous Australian airman of the 1920s and '30s.

Car culture

Most Sydneysiders learn to drive while they are teenagers and many families have two or more cars. As a result, Sydney has a serious traffic problem. Sydney Harbour Tunnel was opened in 1992 to ease pressure on Sydney Harbour Bridge. **Expressways** were built to improve traffic flow. But as the 21st century approaches, the city authorities are struggling to reduce traffic jams and air pollution.

ENTERTAINMENT

A magnificent arts centre stands at Sydney's heart – the Opera House. But the city also has many other wonderful theatres, as well as hundreds of street entertainers. And Sydney is a great place to watch almost every kind of sport.

▲ An orchestra performs in the concert hall of the Sydney Opera House. The rings that hang above their heads improve the sound quality.

At the opera

Many people go to Sydney Opera House to see opera in the specially designed theatre. There is much more on offer too. The Sydney Symphony Orchestra gives frequent performances in the 2,690-seat concert hall. The Drama Theatre hosts the productions of the Sydney Theatre Company, many by Australian writer David Williamson, while the smaller Playhouse often shows plays from abroad. The Australian Ballet and the Sydney Dance Company, a modern dance group, also perform in the Opera House. There are about 3,000 shows of all sorts in the complex every year.

Theatre time

Sydney's oldest theatre is the Theatre Royal. It was founded in 1833 by Barnett Levey, 'the father of Australian theatre', and is still open. The richly decorated State Theatre, with its marble staircase, glittering chandeliers and Wurlitzer organ, opened in 1929 as a grand picture palace (cinema). Now it shows films throughout the year and hosts the Sydney Film Festival in June. It also has live entertainment, particularly musicals.

▼ Film-lovers can watch the stars on a vast screen at Darling Harbour's new IMAX cinema.

MODERN MUSIC

People who prefer rock and pop to classical music have plenty of choice in Sydney. A variety of famous bands plays at Sydney Entertainment Centre. It is the largest music venue in the city, holding up to 12,000 people. Another place to see the stars is the State Theatre, while new bands look for their big break at the Annandale Hotel and other pubs.

▲ Large crowds attend both one-day contests and Test Matches lasting up to five days at Sydney Cricket Ground.

Sports scene

Sydneysiders love to play all kinds of sport. They also have many opportunities to watch the professionals. International cricket matches are held at Sydney Cricket Ground. **Australian Rules Football** is also played here, and rugby league at the nearby Sydney Sports Stadium is very popular. Horse racing is a passion for many in Sydney. Randwick is the most famous of the city's four racecourses and over 50 meetings a year are held there.

MUSEUMS AND ART GALLERIES

Sydney is packed with museums, including one devoted to the city itself. There are plenty of galleries, too, where art-lovers can spend hours gazing at everything from Aboriginal **acrylics** to Picassos.

▲ This sculpture, *Edge of the Trees*, stands outside the Museum of Sydney. Two artists, one of them Aborigine, made it together.

The Museum of Sydney

The Museum of Sydney stands on the site of the old Government House, where New South Wales' first eight governors lived. Its exhibits tell the story of the city from 1788 to 1850, from the point of view of both Iora Aborigines and European settlers. Special features include recordings of Iora tales by modern Aborigines and a 33-screen video bank that extends from top to bottom of the three-storey building.

The Australian Museum

This natural history museum focuses on the wildlife of Australia and the Pacific region, whether extinct or still living. It houses displays of all sorts of creatures, as well as many skeletons, including 'Eric' the **plesiosaur**. The museum also has an important Aboriginal collection, but visitors need to make an appointment to see its rarest items.

ELIZABETH BAY HOUSE

The beautiful Elizabeth Bay House, completed in 1838, stands in the suburb of Kings Cross. The architect was John Verge, who designed the building for Alexander Macleay, then the Colonial Secretary of New South Wales. Macleay spent so much money on his mansion that he went bankrupt and had to move out. In 1977 the house became a museum, and was re-furnished. Visitors can explore the upstairs rooms and the cellars.

This acrylic painting by Aboriginal artist Clifford Possum Tjapaltjarri hangs in the Yiribana Gallery. ➤

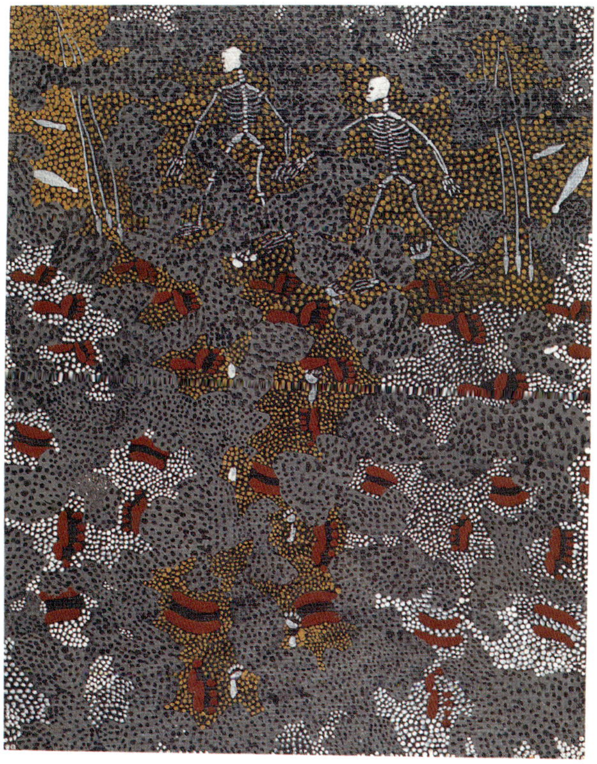

The Powerhouse Museum

The award-winning Powerhouse Museum, in a former power station, is the largest in Australia. The main themes of the museum are science and technology. Other subjects, including Australian life, are also covered in its five areas. Among the many exhibits are a steam engine and a flying boat suspended from the ceiling. There are also hands-on displays that make science fun.

The Powerhouse Museum contains ▲ this wonderful steam train. It was the first ever to run in New South Wales.

Art galleries

The Art Gallery of New South Wales displays paintings by Australian artists such as Sidney Nolan, and a few works by major European names such as Picasso. The Yiribana Gallery, which opened within the main gallery in 1994, contains more than 200 examples of Aboriginal and Torres Strait Islander art (from the Torres Strait, off the coast of North-East Australia). These works include sculptures and bark paintings. The gallery also has Asian art and stunning photographs.

Harbourside art

The Museum of Contemporary Art (see page 42) was opened on the harbourside in 1991. It was funded with money left by an Australian art collector called John Wardell Power, who died in 1943. Australia's best collection of modern art, including works by Andy Warhol and Roy Lichtenstein, is displayed there.

SHOPS AND MARKETS

People can buy almost anything in the shops and markets of modern Sydney, from clothes by top international designers to Australian art. There is a huge array of goods on offer, and more tourists shop in the city than go to the Sydney Opera House.

▲ Sydney's Strand Arcade is a 19th-century shopping complex that has been restored for modern use. It was built in 1892.

Shopping centres

The Queen Victoria Building is one of the oldest shopping centres in Sydney. It was built in 1898 as a market, then served as a library, a warehouse and offices before falling into disrepair. In the 1980s it was returned to its former glory. Now there are over 200 shops and restaurants under its copper domes. Its Victorian windows, cast-iron staircase and lift have all been restored. The nearby Skygarden is a modern shopping precinct. It sells expensive designer goods and has a café and restaurant under its glass roof.

▲ The huge, glittering perfume department at David Jones. The store was refitted in the 1980s.

Department stores

Sydney has two main department stores: Grace Bros and David Jones. The more up-market is David Jones, which calls itself 'the most beautiful store in the world'. It opened in the mid-19th century on one site, but now fills two separate buildings. The Elizabeth Street branch is the place to buy expensive clothes, perfume and cosmetics. It is also known for its beautiful window displays at Christmas and flower displays in the spring. The Market Street branch's main attraction is its splendid food hall.

Sydney Fish Market

Sydney Fish Market attracts both expert fishmongers and ordinary seafood-lovers. Early in the day, professionals bid for the amazing range of marine and freshwater creatures on offer. Some are then sold in market shops. Blue swimmer crabs, Sydney Harbour prawns and **barramundi** are just a few of the edible delights that tempt the crowds.

More than 100 types of fish are on sale at Sydney Fish Market. Here, a trader prepares slices of raw tuna. ▲

AUSTRALIANA

Australiana – typically Australian goods – are among the most commonly purchased items in Sydney shops. They include opals, kangaroo-skin rugs, macadamia nuts and Aboriginal arts and crafts like this sculpture (below right). Traditional clothing is popular, too. Shops stock the felt hats, oilskin coats and **moleskin** trousers worn by rugged Australian farmers.

General markets

There are many general markets in Sydney, each with its own character. Among the best is the Paddington Bazaar, which takes place every Saturday. Goods for sale include fashionable clothes, pottery and silver jewellery. Paddy's Market is held in an undercover site near Darling Harbour. It opened in 1869, making it the city's oldest market. With about 1,000 stalls, it is also the largest. Food, flowers, clothes, electrical goods, even pets can be bought under its vast roof.

FOOD AND DRINK

At the time when most people in Sydney were British or Irish, the food was plain and stodgy – a typical meal was meat pie, tomato sauce and mashed potato. Immigrants from China, Italy, Greece and elsewhere have transformed eating and drinking in the city. Now, at home and in restaurants, a huge range of delicious dishes is prepared.

▲ Sydneysiders enjoy barbecues in their gardens, on beaches or in the city's parks.

BUSH TUCKER

Foods traditionally eaten by Aborigines include crocodiles, wallabies and **witchetty grubs**, as well as a variety of rainforest fruits (above). Now this food, sometimes known as bush tucker, is making its way into Sydney restaurants. At Edna's Table you can eat these foods in a room decorated with Aboriginal art, and sometimes watch Aboriginal dancers.

Home cooking

Plenty of locally produced fresh food is available in Sydney. There is fish and shellfish, as well as lamb and other meats from nearby farms. Fruits, vegetables and cheeses from elsewhere in Australia are on offer, as well as imported foods. The range is increasing. Before 1993, for example, it was illegal to eat kangaroo, but now it often appears on meat counters. Sydneysiders cook everything from roast joints with potatoes to pizzas and Thai curries. They often barbecue steaks, chicken, sausages, prawns and octopus.

Café society

Italian immigrants set up the first real cafés in Sydney and now there are hundreds, especially in the inner suburb of Darlinghurst. The most famous is the Italian-run Bar Coluzzi, which serves a specially blended coffee and delicious snacks. The city's best-loved café is a more down-to-earth establishment. Harry's Café de Wheels is nothing more than a caravan in Woolloomooloo, near the Botanic Gardens. It was set up in 1945 to sell old-style Australian food and still does today. One of its most popular dishes is the Pie Floater – meat pie drifting on a sea of pea soup.

▲ This Doyles seafood restaurant is in Circular Quay, central Sydney. People eating here have a wonderful view across the harbour.

▲ Hungry Sydneysiders cluster around Harry's Café de Wheels. Many people come here after a night on the town.

Restaurant meals

Today, there are about 2,000 restaurants in Sydney. Some of the best specialize in seafood. Doyles in Watsons Bay (see page 18) was among the first to begin this trend, in 1885. It sells freshly cooked fish and chips that customers can eat while gazing out over the harbour. Rockpool in the Rocks is the place for gourmet dishes. There, people can eat fish such as fresh tuna cooked with Asian herbs and spices. This mixed style of cooking is known as Modern Australian.

SPECIAL EVENTS

There are special activities to enjoy during every one of Sydney's seasons, from high summer to the depths of winter.

▼ Sydneysiders on Australia Day, dressed in 18th-century naval uniforms, re-enact the arrival of Captain Arthur Phillip.

Summer celebrations

The month-long Sydney Festival starts the year with a bang. Every January, when the weather is hottest, there are open-air events across the city. The climax is on 26 January, Australia Day. People commemorate the arrival of Captain Phillip (see pages 8-9) and the birth of Sydney with celebrations including a concert in The Domain and fireworks in Darling Harbour. Chinatown is extra lively in late January or early February, at Chinese New Year. Lion dancers wear colourful costumes, while firecrackers explode around them.

Large, colourful kites soar above Bondi Beach during September's Festival of the Winds. ▼

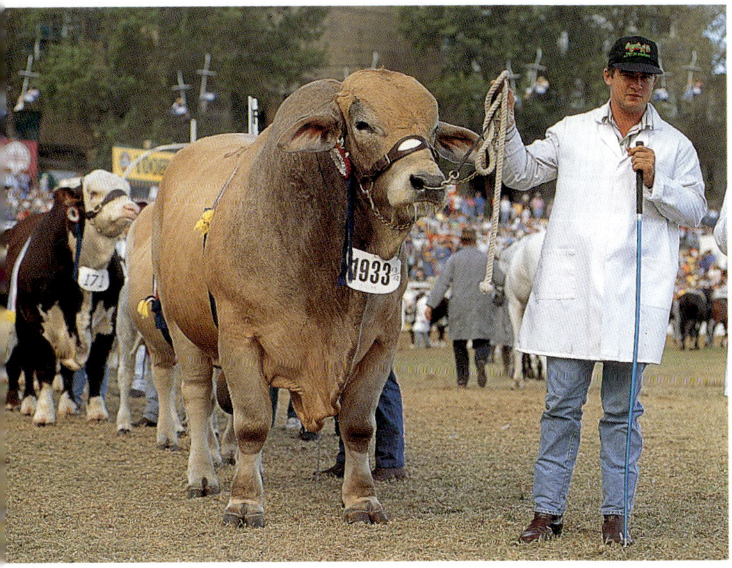

◄ Sydneysiders have a chance to meet the farmers of New South Wales at the Royal Easter Show. They can watch show-jumping and prize cattle or admire the giant pumpkins and vegetables.

Autumn events

There are two spectacular street events in March. On the first Saturday of the month, Sydney's Gay and Lesbian **Mardi Gras** Parade takes place. About 400,000 gay people live in the city and many more arrive from all over the world to join them in this extravagant carnival. On St Patrick's Day (17 March), the city's Irish population celebrates with another massive street parade that winds slowly through the city.

Winter and spring

The Film Festival in June is a major event in the Sydney winter. But people who prefer keeping fit to sitting in a cinema have plenty to keep them busy as well. Almost anyone with enough enthusiasm can run the 14-km City to Surf Race from the Town Hall to Bondi Beach. The 42-km Sydney Marathon gives professional athletes the chance to show how it should be done. Both races are in August. As spring arrives in September, Bondi Beach hosts an unusual special event. During the Festival of the Winds, people fly their kites to create a sensational display.

CHRISTMAS AND NEW YEAR

Sydney hosts two major open-air events over Christmas. On Christmas Day thousands of people, usually tourists, go to Bondi Beach for a festive picnic. On Boxing Day, crowds gather in Sydney Harbour to watch the start of the Sydney to Hobart Yacht Race (below). Only expert sailors attempt this voyage to the capital of Tasmania. New Year's Eve is the occasion for another celebration. Parties go on all night and dazzling firework displays light up the sky.

CITY CHARACTERS

Since Sydney was founded, it has been home to an array of colourful characters. Many have made a lasting mark on its history.

Francis Greenway

Francis Greenway worked as an architect in Bristol. He was sentenced to death for forging a contract, but was then transported to the Sydney **penal colony**. Two years after his arrival he became a government architect. By 1822 he had designed 40 buildings, including St James' Church and Hyde Park Barracks (see pages 14-15). Later the British government sacked him for extravagance.

After losing his job, Francis Greenway soon lost all his money too. He died penniless in 1837. His grave is unmarked.

Joan Sutherland

Opera singer Joan Sutherland was born in Sydney in 1926 and first appeared on stage there in 1951. She went to London to study at the Royal College of Music and to sing at the Royal Opera House. Sutherland has performed at opera houses around the world, including the Metropolitan in New York. Her beautiful soprano voice won her great praise. She retired in 1990.

Joan Sutherland, dressed for a major operatic role. She often sang Italian operas by composers such as Vincenzo Bellini.

▼ Patrick White's novels include *Voss* (1957). It is based on the true story of Ludwig Leichhardt, a man who explored the Australian deserts.

Patrick White

The writer Patrick White was born to Australian parents in London in 1912. He grew up in both Australia and England, but in 1948 settled in Sydney and became a full-time author. The themes of his work include the trials of Australia's early settlers and the shallowness of Sydneysiders. In 1973 White won the Nobel Prize for Literature.

Pat O'Shane

Pat O'Shane was born in the **state** of Queensland, north of New South Wales, but Sydney has long been her home. She was the first Aborigine to qualify as a lawyer and in 1976 became a barrister. Ten years later she was also made a magistrate. In the 1980s O'Shane ran the Aboriginal Affairs Department of the New South Wales government. She is a **republican** and in 1998 took part in the convention that helped to decide how Australia will be governed if it ends its links with Britain (see pages 42-43).

SYDNEY STARS

Two Hollywood stars have links with Sydney. Paul Hogan grew up in the city and worked as a maintenance man on Sydney Harbour Bridge. He entered a television talent contest and never looked back. The film *Crocodile Dundee* (1986) brought him world fame. Mel Gibson (right), the leading actor in films such as *Mad Max* (1979) and *Lethal Weapon* (1987), is Australian, although he was born in the USA. He studied at the National Institute of Dramatic Art in Sydney.

SYDNEY'S FUTURE

The future event most on Sydneysiders' minds at the moment is the Olympic Games (see box) and the changes they are bringing to the city. Many everyday changes are also taking place that will probably have an even greater impact on Sydney life.

▼ Many old buildings are being renovated. This office block now houses the Museum of Contemporary Art.

People power

Sydney's population mix is constantly altering. In recent years, the largest number of new Sydneysiders has come from countries such as Vietnam, Indonesia, Malaysia and the Philippines. The Chinese community is also growing fast and Chinese is the second most widely spoken language in the city, after English. People from Sydney's many cultures now influence all areas of life, particularly trade, education and politics, and they are gradually changing the nature of the city.

Building the future

Sydney is a city of suburbs. But now developers are creating new homes in converted city-centre tower blocks and warehouses. They are also renovating run-down inner suburbs such as Surry Hills to attract people there. This policy can bring life and money to dying areas, but it can also force the original residents to leave (see page 21). Other new buildings in Sydney include the Aquamagic Film and Laser Spectacular in Darling Harbour and a vast complex for Sydney Harbour Casino.

▲ When Queen Elizabeth II visited Australia in 1992, she was its head of state. She may not keep that role for much longer.

Causes for celebration

Like everyone else, Sydneysiders will celebrate the arrival of the year 2000. They also have the Olympics to celebrate, as well as Australia's 100th birthday in 2001 (see pages 10-11). The city is likely to host some wonderful parties in the near future.

The wider world

Changes in Australia will also affect Sydney. In 1999 Australians will vote on whether their country should become a republic. If they approve this, the British monarch will no longer be Australia's **head of state.** Whatever happens, in future the country is likely to have less contact with Britain and more with nearby **Asia-Pacific countries.**

THE SYDNEY OLYMPICS

Sydney hosts both the Olympic and the **Paralympic Games** in the year 2000. The main site of the games is the 760-hectare Sydney Olympic Park in Homebush Bay, west of the city. Facilities such as the Sydney International Aquatic Centre are already open. A 110,000-seat stadium and the gymnastics arena will be completed in 1999. The Sydney Olympics aim to be the first environmentally-friendly Olympic Games. Newington, the athletes' village, will be solar-powered. Even the Olympic mascots – an **echidna** called Millie, a **kookaburra** called Olly and a platypus called Syd – have an environmental theme. They represent earth, air and water.

Sydney's new Star City complex is like a mini Las Vegas, containing a casino as well as fashionable shops. ▲

TIMELINE

This timeline shows some of the most important dates in Sydney's history. All the events are mentioned earlier in the book.

BC

c.40,000 years ago
Aborigines reach Australia from South-East Asia

c.20,000 years ago
Aborigines settle in Sydney Harbour area

18TH CENTURY

1770
Captain James Cook lands in Botany Bay, claims Australia's east coast for Britain and names it New South Wales

1786
British government decides to set up a ***penal colony*** *in Botany Bay*

1787
First Fleet, led by Captain Arthur Phillip, sets sail from Britain

1788
First Fleet arrives in Sydney and Captain Phillip founds settlement

1790
Second Fleet arrives in Sydney

19TH CENTURY

1810-1821
Lachlan Macquarie is Governor of New South Wales

1813
Explorers cross Blue Mountains west of Sydney

1814
Francis Greenway arrives in Sydney

1816
Cadman's Cottage completed

1819
Hyde Park Barracks completed

1820
St James' Church completed

1833
Theatre Royal, Sydney's first theatre, opens

1838
Elizabeth Bay House completed

1840
British government stops sending criminals to New South Wales

1842
Sydney becomes a city

1850
Sydney University founded

1851
Gold discovered west of Blue Mountains; gold rush begins

1855
Parliament set up in Sydney

1856
Sydney becomes capital of New South Wales colony
Royal Botanic Gardens founded

1858
Sydney Observatory built

1869
Paddy's Market opens

1885
Doyles restaurant opens in Watsons Bay

1887
Customs House built

1888
Sydney celebrates its centenary

1889
Town Hall built
1890
Economic ***depression*** *hits Sydney*
1892
Strand Arcade opens
1898
Queen Victoria Building opens

20TH CENTURY

1900
112 people die following an outbreak of plague
1901
Australia formed
Sydney becomes capital of New South Wales ***state***
1914-18
Many Sydneysiders fight in the ***First World War****, particularly at Gallipoli (1915-16)*
1916
Taronga Zoo opens
1929
State Theatre opens
1930s
Economic depression hits Sydney
1932
Sydney Harbour Bridge opens
1939-45
Many Sydneysiders fight in the ***Second World War***
1942
Japanese submarines sail into Sydney harbour and are sunk
1945
Harry's Café de Wheels opens
1947
Post-war immigration begins
1960s
Asian immigrants begin to arrive in Australia
1973
Sydney Opera House opens
Lebanese people begin to arrive in Australia
1980s
Gang warfare breaks out in Sydney
1981
Sydney Tower completed
1988
Sydney celebrates its bi-centenary
Sydney Convention and Exhibition Centre opens
1989
Australian government publishes its National Agenda for a Multicultural Australia
1990s
Many Hong Kong Chinese people arrive in Australia
1991
Royal Commission *report on police treatment of Aborigines published*
Museum of Contemporary Art opens
1992
Sydney Harbour Tunnel opens
1993
It becomes legal to eat kangaroo meat in Australia
1994
New third runway opens at Kingsford Smith Airport
Yiribana Gallery opens in Art Gallery of New South Wales
1999
Australians vote on whether Australia should become a republic

21ST CENTURY

2000
Sydney will host the Olympic and ***Paralympic Games***
2001
Australia will celebrate its 200th birthday

GLOSSARY

acrylic A work of art created with acrylic paints made from a chemical called acrylic acid. Acrylic paints are used by many modern Aboriginal artists.

Anglican Belonging to the Church of England or an associated church.

Asia-Pacific countries Asian countries that lie in or border the Pacific Ocean, particularly its southern section. They include Japan, Indonesia and Malaysia.

Australian Rules Football A type of football that is a mixture of rugby, Gaelic (Irish) football and ordinary football. Teams have 18 players each. They play with an oval ball on an oval pitch.

barramundi A type of Australian freshwater fish with a long, scaly body and large, wide fins.

Central Business District The central area of a city where the major businesses are based. Every Australian city has a Central Business District, or CBD for short.

charge room A room in a police station where prisoners are formally accused of their crimes.

Conservatorium The Australian word for an advanced school or college of music. The British term is usually 'conservatoire'.

container ships Large ships that carry cargo packed in standard-sized containers.

crude petroleum Oil that has not yet been refined to make petrol or paraffin, but remains in its natural state.

depression (economic) A time of low business growth, high unemployment and falling prices.

echidna A spine-covered animal with a long, thin nose and powerful claws. Echidnas eat ants and termites, which is why they are also called spiny anteaters.

ethnic Racial; relating to people from a certain race.

expressway A motorway designed to carry fast traffic through a city or town.

extended family A family that contains not only parents and their children but also grandparents, aunts, uncles etc.

federation A country or other political unit in which power is shared between several regional governments and a single national government.

First World War A major war that lasted from 1914 to 1918 and involved many countries. Australians fought alongside the British, French, Russians (until 1917) and Americans (from 1917) to defeat Germany, Austria-Hungary and their allies.

gable A triangular section of an outside house wall between the sloping ends of an overhanging roof.

Governor-General The high-ranking official whose job it is to represent the British king or queen in Australia.

Greenwich Mean Time The time in Greenwich, England, which stands on the zero line of longitude. It is used as a base for calculating the time in the rest of the world.

head of state The official head of a country. Many heads of state, including the British queen, do not have much real political power.

Herbarium A collection of dried plants. The National Herbarium of New South Wales is also a centre for the study of Australian plants.

kookaburra A type of grey Australian kingfisher that lives in trees. It is famous for its strange call that sounds rather like laughter. Another name for this bird is 'laughing jackass'.

Mardi Gras The French term for Shrove Tuesday, and the name given to a festival celebrated in some countries on or around that day. Shrove Tuesday occurs just before Lent, a period of 40 days in which many Christians used to fast or give up certain foods. On Shrove Tuesday they ate rich foods and had fun before the fasting began. Now most people join in the celebrations without fasting afterwards.

moleskin A type of strong cotton fabric.

monorail A single-track railway that is usually raised above the ground.

Paralympic Games A major games and athletics meeting at which disabled people compete.

pavilion A decorative building that provides shelter but is usually open to the outside.

penal colony A place where criminals are sent to be punished.

plaster casts Moulds made from plaster of Paris, a type of white powder that sets solid.

plesiosaur A type of reptile that lived in the sea millions of years ago. Plesiosaurs had long necks and paddle-like limbs. They could grow to a length of 12 metres.

prospectors People who search for gold and other precious metals in the ground, rivers etc.

quadrangle A four-sided, usually rectangular courtyard surrounded by buildings.

regatta A series of yacht and other boat races.

republican A person who believes that countries should be governed only by elected rulers and should not have kings or queens.

reserve An area of land set aside for a particular group of people in order to separate them from others.

Royal Commission A group of people selected by the government to enquire into a serious issue and to work out a plan of action. It is called a 'Royal' Commission as Queen Elizabeth II is the Australian head of state.

Second World War A major war that lasted from 1939 to 1945 and involved many countries. Australians joined with the British, French, Russians and Americans (from 1941) to defeat Germany, Italy and their allies.

state A country or other political unit that governs itself and makes its own laws. Australia is divided into six states. One of these is New South Wales, and Sydney is its capital.

Triads Secret societies of Chinese criminals. Triads are often involved in large-scale crimes such as drug-smuggling and gambling. They operate in many countries outside China.

witchetty grubs The caterpillars of an Australian moth. Aborigines eat the grubs both cooked and raw.

INDEX